MINE
for a
TIME

By
Coretta H. Collins

Cover designed by AviLuxe Designs

Printed in the United States of America
First Printing: June 2022
The Scribe Tribe Publishing Group

THE SCRIBE TRIBE
PUBLISHING GROUP

ISBN – 978-1-958436-09-7

There's a hole in my heart where joy used to be.
There's a hole in my heart where anticipation resided.
There's a hole in my heart where hope bubbled over.
There's a hole in my heart where you used to be.
I will not get over it but I will get through it.

Coretta Collins

This book is a collection of poems and narratives for people who have been impacted by pregnancy loss or early infant loss including miscarriage, ectopic pregnancy and stillbirth. It is for you, the parent grieving through your loss experience. It is for you, the mother, father, sister, brother, cousin or friend of the grieving parents. It is for anyone who would like to better understand what a person suffering from pregnancy and early infant loss is going through in order to provide substantial and positive support.

The emotions and grief process during pregnancy or infant loss is unique and filled with uncertainty. It is my prayer that you find the content of this book relatable and encouraging. I also pray that through relating to the content that you find the strength to go on and that you will overcome. May you find healing and wholeness as you recover from your loss but also give yourself the patience and grace to work through it. I know that you will not get over it, but I pray that you will get through it.

In memory of our beautiful baby boy, Walter Eron Collins. You were mine for a time. Until we meet again...

Table of Contents

Emotional Rollercoaster

My loss was totally unexpected. We had no idea of what was coming. I am not sure that knowing would have made the experience any easier so it does not matter. I felt blindsided. I felt robbed. I felt lost. All of these emotions took a heavy toll on my heart, my mind and my soul. My emotional state became fragile, volatile even. I was all over the place emotionally yet nowhere at all. I wanted to talk. I didn't want to talk. I wanted to cry. I didn't want to cry. I was mad. I was sad. I prayed. I cussed. I slept. I stayed awake. I ate. I didn't eat. I still felt pregnant. I even forgot sometimes that I wasn't. Actually, I thought that I felt him move even though I was no longer pregnant. Nevertheless, I persevered. And I made it. It is a miracle. It was God.

God, family and friends that helped me make it through. I am resilient. You are too. Give yourself grace. You will get to a place where the emotions will not make you feel like you are losing your mind. You will persevere.

Don't Ask

Don't ask me how I'm doing
I just buried my baby, my child, my son.
Don't ask me how I'm doing
Wondering what my world may become.

Don't ask me how I'm doing
My emotions run deep to the core.
Don't ask me how I'm doing
I feel I can't take it anymore.

When asking how I'm doing
Do you REALLY want to know?
Well imagine yourself in my shoes
If it was your son who had to go.

When asking how I'm doing
What do you expect me to say?

My heart is broken, mind distorted...
Me telling you could take all day.

The question "How are you doing?"
Has become so cliché.
We do it out of habit
Expecting a fine, alright, okay.

However, what if by chance,
I told you my life story.
About the child I loved, cherished and carried for 8 months...
About how he's gone to glory.

What if I really took the time
To tell you my thoughts, dreams and fears.
Would you really have the time
To try to comfort me through my tears.

Don't ask me how I'm doing
Please think of something else to say.
If you indeed REALLY want to be there for me
You'll decide on another way.

Don't ask me how I'm doing
The truth is, I'm not sure
I can't see past the pain right now
But somehow I will endure.

RoLleR cOaStEr

I'm not in *Georgia*, but I'm in a *Cyclone*,
"One day at a time," my new favorite song.

And I don't need a *Machine* to make me *Scream*,
With emotions going up and down, what more is there to need?

Yes, indeed this is a *Mind Bender*,
With loops and turns, hills and valleys clogging up my center.

I know that this is my *Thunder River* and I do let *Splash
Water Fall*,
But thank God for His Son, my husband, family and friends
who are there when I call.

Sometimes my *Mind Train* gets off track,
But Lord have mercy! He pulls it right back.

And even though my life's a *Scorcher*
I know I'll be blessed in the midst of my torture.

And when I feel like I am ***Batman***
Blind and in the dark, God has the plan.

Cuz he is a ***Ninja*** in His own right,
All of my battles He has to fight.

And when that ***Viper*** comes in to devour,
He gives me strength no matter the hour.

Acrophobia? *Not my God*; He ***Freely Falls*** to uplift me.
He's better than ***Superman*** could ever be.

So no matter how wavering my ROLLER coaster may be,
This is all a process that leads to a better me.

And at those times when my car is going uphill,
I will rejoice and be thankful and just sit still.

So when it starts to descend back down
And once again I feel lower than the ground,

I'll have my moment, cuz that's all it will be,
I won't let the devil get the best of me.

But knowing this is a process and things are still fresh,
I'll keep looking up in the midst of my distress.

For there will come a day when my ROLLER COASTER
will rest,
And He'll say, "Well-done daughter, you've passed the test!"

Then the day will come when I'll enter in,
And I'll see my son Walter and hold him again.

I've Never...

Excuse me if I seem dumbfounded
Because my mind is very clouded

I've never buried my child before
And after this, I hope not anymore

Forgive me for asking a lot of questions
But what's going on inside me surpasses combustion

So you tell me you need to take him to the hospital morgue
Well take me too, I never buried my child before

What do you mean decide on a funeral home
I still can't believe my son is really gone

What do you mean the funeral home will come and get him
Well if he has to go, why can't I just take him to them

Pick out a casket according to his size
He's a baby, how much could it take to decide

Bring back an outfit for him to wear
Well forgive my shock, I don't mean to just stare

But I've never buried my child before
And after this, I pray not anymore

Choose a date, a place, a time
I expected him to do this for mine

You tell me to expect the death certificate in the mail
He has to be in heaven, because for me this is hell

Decide on a vault company I want to use,
Well you tell me, why should I have to choose

You see, I've never buried my child before
And after this, I pray not anymore

Then there's an obituary that needs to be written
I'm in a state of shock, you've got to be kidding

You tell me to come view my son to be sure things are up to par
Unless he has arisen, "up to par" is very far

You tell me he looks nice and everything turned out well
He's deceased and in a casket as far as I can tell

There's nothing nice about this and that's just how I feel
But of course not, I'm his mother and you couldn't
understand for real

You see I've never buried my child before
And I hope after this, not anymore!

I Cry

I cry because it somehow eases my pain

I cry because it somehow lifts the burden if only for a moment

I cry because it's the cleansing of my heart

I cry because it's the opening of my soul

I cry because sometimes the sadness overwhelms me

I cry because sometimes the pain pierces deep within

I cry because the anger searches for a means of escape

I cry because I can't go around screaming all the time

I cry because he never had the chance to

I cry because all I ever wanted was for him to be able to

I cry because it's the only thing I can do

So I cry.

Finding the right words to say when someone is grieving can be beyond challenging. What can be even harder is saying nothing at all but really sometimes the silence is all you need.

Sit

You don't have to say anything
I know it's hard
Your presence fills the void
Your words can not

Just sit with me here
You don't have to talk
The words from your mouth
Won't heal my broken heart

Sit here with me
The silence may be deafening
But you're doing your part
Whether you feel like it or not

Just sit down with me
Feeling your presence gives me some peace
It lets me know that you really love me

Sit for a while
Let me stare into space
Or cry on your shoulder
Whatever the case

In your mind, I know you're struggling with what words to say
But just sit with me a while
Say nothing
It's okay

You sitting with me gives comfort
I didn't know I needed
Sitting without expectations
Helps ease my grief

Please don't make me talk
Just sit with me here

Over time the moment will come
When we'll find words again

Sit with me now
That's all I want for you to do
Sit with me through this
It may not seem like it
But it's the best of you.

Mine for a Time

I've known you for many months now,
To live without you, I'll have to learn how.

You were mine for a time, you just couldn't stay,
Because God saw fit to take you away.

I can still feel your kicks, your squirms and wiggles,
Just feeling you inside me, made me giggle.

I learned your ways, like when you wanted to eat,
Loved watching you grow and hearing your heartbeat.

But we'll meet again and then we'll play,
You were mine for a time but God had the last say.

Lord knows I love you and I wish you'd stayed here,
You were mine for a time, but the angels needed you dear.

ALL THE STAGES

I remember feeling all the stages of grief at once and then none at all. I was a bottle of emotions yet none at all. It seems like there should be another name for it. Grief just doesn't seem like an entirely adequate description. The stages of grief are denial, anger, bargaining, depression and acceptance. Some days, I felt more of one stage than another. Some days, I wished that I could feel nothing. The pain is so devastating and deep. In the end though, no amount of denial, anger, bargaining or depression was going to bring back my baby boy. However, acceptance takes time. Though, I still wonder if it is truly acceptance or just dealing with it. Go through your stages; work through your stages. It is normal. You are normal. Your grief is real. Your feelings are real. In time, you will heal.

Grief-*n*. the anguish experienced after significant loss, usually the death of a beloved person. Grief is often distinguished from bereavement and mourning. Not all bereavements result in a strong grief response, and not all grief is given public expression (disenfranchised grief). Grief often includes physiological distress, separation anxiety, confusion, yearning, obsessive dwelling on the past, and apprehension about the future. Intense grief can become life-threatening through disruption of the immune system, self-neglect, and suicidal thoughts. Grief may also take the form of regret for something lost, remorse for something done, or sorrow for a mishap to oneself. (APA Dictionary of Psychology)

GRIEF...

You're in shock, disbelief, can't believe what's happened...
You finally start to grasp it, you think...
No you just can't believe it happened...

You cry, you moan, you sigh...
You holler, you scream, you die...
Not physical death in the way we know it...
But mentally, emotionally you're dead, you can hold it...

Guilt comes, it goes...
Anger comes, it goes...
Resentment comes, it goes...
Bitterness comes, it goes...
Frustration comes, it goes...
Sadness comes, it goes...
Loneliness comes, it goes...
And then too, smiles come, they go...

Laughter comes, it goes...
Joy comes, it goes...

But no matter how far it goes it always comes back.

Grief...the roller coaster ride no one wants to take
The journey, the trip, the sojourn no one wants to make.

Yet it's a part of life
Though you feel you can do without
Yet the process is yours to go through
Though it's nothing you dreamt about...

Stillbirth is Still Birth

<u>Stillbirth</u> is <u>Still</u> <u>Birth</u>
He once had life do not minimize its worth

He <u>Still</u> made his journey down the <u>Birth</u> canal
An everlasting impression on my heart he will have

He once squirmed and kicked, like everybody else
Yes, I know he lived, I witnessed it myself

So what if he never saw *our* light of day
He did within me, in his on way

So what if he never uttered a sound or breathed *our* fresh air
He never really had to, he had what he needed in me, in there

And so what if he was <u>Still</u> when he was <u>Born</u>
He <u>Still</u> lived and lives in me, for he is <u>Still</u> my son

So what if he was <u>Still</u>, upon entrance into this earth
He once was not <u>Still</u> for he once did live and to him I <u>Still</u>
gave <u>Birth</u>

So my <u>Still</u> son was <u>Still</u> <u>Born</u> and to me that is <u>Still</u> <u>Birth</u>
Not in the sense others may see it, but I value his life's worth

So does my son have a <u>Birth</u> certificate?
No, just a death one and I must deal with it

But <u>Stillbirth</u> is <u>Still</u> <u>Birth</u> to me. It may seem strange to you.
But that's fine if it does because I know in my heart it's true.

J.J. Therapy

I finally held my first baby today
Marvin Jr., better known as J.J.

I was happy; it was exciting and fun
I finally did something I wasn't sure could be done

I thought that I'd be sad and overwhelmed with tears
But I ended up having joy and a ray of cheer

It was indeed a big step that I chose to make
A great leap of faith I had to take

Though in the back of my mind, I thought of Walter Eron
Somehow spending time with J.J. made me feel closer to my son

Being with J.J. was comforting for me
I realized that he is indeed great therapy

For what a difference a day can make
When prior thoughts of babies made my heart ache

New signs of healing, new signs of pressing on
Maybe learning to accept my son is where he belongs

So glad it was something I'm now able to do
This J.J. therapy may sure help me through

I thank that little man, for he'll never know how much
I appreciate holding him, feeding him and feeling his
warm touch

Reignited passion in me that I am too still a mother
Gave me inspiration to believe I can have Walter a sister
and brother

Only two months old and already a therapist
Well son, thanks for my session, I truly cherish it!

SURVIVE

It occurred to me the other day
That survival is the only way

It's the only sane option I can take
The only reasonable decision I can make

The truth of the matter is I have to admit the facts
My son is gone and I can't have him back

It is not something that can be rescinded
Though if it were possible, I'd be first to recommend it

Sure I could exterminate myself
But what would that do for me and to everybody else

Besides the Holy Spirit in me knows that's not the way
And when the devil tries to defeat me, I know I have to pray

So you see, that puts me back at Point A
And reassures me more and more that survival is the only way

For I must live as God wants me to
I can't change what has happened and neither can you

I must find peace within my heart
I guess accepting the truth is a great start

So my son's in heaven and he's not going to return
So surviving is my only alternative, so this I'll have to learn

I'll never ever "get over it" for this is my dear child
But to live, I must survive it, though it could take a while

Yes, this is my son; I can't ever "get over it"
But with the help of God, I can, I must survive it!

Sad, Angry, Selfish
S.A.S.

I'm selfish and I know it
Got the bitterness to show it

Angry as I want to be
Can't believe this has happened to me

Melancholy, sad, even sort of depressed
No way I want to believe this was for the best

Say what you want, but my son should be with me
I mean that with the utmost sincerity

Spare me the speech about how Heaven's a better place
Don't you think I know that, I know God for goodness sake

Doesn't mean I have to like it, for God and I do disagree
But I know He's sovereign and He loves and cares for me

Though I must be honest, this was a strange way of showing it
But I trust You have a plan even if I do not know it

And please don't bother telling me everything happens for a reason
That still doesn't change the fact that this feels like treason

And you don't have to tell me that God knows best
If I didn't know that, I'd be in a even bigger mess

The fact is that I know God has a purpose and a plan
Though it doesn't mean I'm happy that it involved using my
little man

For I'm selfish and I'm angry and I'm sad
Will ask God what He was thinking when He designed the plan He had

I wanted my dear son to be here with me
For him to see *me* off into eternity.

PHYSICAL PROMISES

While I was pregnant, I often imagined what our baby would look like. Would he look just like my husband? Would he have any of my characteristics? It was always amazing to see him during the ultrasounds. Some features were already apparent. When I had him he was a vision of love. He looked like his dad. That much was apparent already. He had the cutest little nose, but my favorite feature was his toes. His toes were like mine and I had never seen tiny toes that looked like mine with the second toe being longer than the big toe. I wondered what his cry would sound like and I wanted to give him a lifetime of kisses. Holding him lifeless in my arms, I realized all of the diminished dreams but I knew my love for him would always remain. Despite the circumstances, I am thankful for the time that we got to spend together as a family before having to part with him. Whether two days, two weeks, twenty weeks or nine months, your baby was yours and you loved him/her and that matters.

Physical Attributes

Long fingers, long toes,
Adorable lips, button nose

Head full of wavy slick hair
Thin eyebrows, little eyelashes, everything's there

Lengthy torso, cute brown ears
And what do you know, a birth mark on the rear

Big brown eyes, I have no doubt
Cute little tongue in your mouth

Wonderfully, Perfectly and Beautifully made
Our boy, our son, Walter Eron
Thanks for the joy you gave

I Never Heard You Cry

I never heard you cry
But I did feel you kick
I never heard you cry
But I did smell your scent

I never heard you cry
But I did hold your hand
I never heard you cry
But you're still my little man

I never heard you cry
But I've felt your hiccups
I never heard you cry
But I did get to pick you up

I never heard you cry
But I did kiss your cheeks
I never heard you cry
But I played with your feet

I never heard you cry
But I did feel you grow
I never heard you cry
But I got prodded by your elbow

I never heard you cry
But I rubbed your little nose
I never heard you cry
But I counted ten fingers and toes

I never heard you cry
But I saw your birthmark on your booty
I never heard you cry
But I witnessed your endless beauty

I never heard you cry
Though I wish some way I could
I never heard you cry
But I know since you're with God, there's no reason why you should

Diminished Dreams or Dreams Deferred?

Though funerals are supposed to be about celebration
I just can't seem to get past the devastation

In the midst of being sad
I find it hard to be glad

That my son's in a better place
Because I'd much rather see his precious face

I find it difficult to celebrate
A life that to me ended too early instead of late

I see aspirations gone down the drain
And anticipation that was in vain

A nursery that is not needed at this time
Toys, crib, clothes and diapers all left behind

No first bath, first laugh or first crawl
No first step, first word or first fall

No growing up, starting school, or having a career
No getting married, being with family, having children to rear

There is no future for my son on this earth
For his had come and gone before I even gave birth

So diminished dreams I now see
Or dreams deferred, for they may come true eventually...

Kiss My Son for Me

Dear Jesus would you please
Give my son a kiss for me

Lean over and kiss his little cheek
And if it's not too much to ask, kiss my favorite little feet

And then when you're done with those precious toes
Go back up and kiss his little button nose

And don't forget to kiss those cute little ears
And take a break to wipe mommy's tears

Then God, if time permits, kiss that little chest
Then raise his head and kiss under his neck

Then give him a zerbert to make him laugh
And a big high five for his dad

Do kiss him for me, if you don't mind
And when I get there I'll make up for lost time.

OUTSIDE OUCHES

It hurts seeing the physical manifestations of your loss. My sweet family had removed all of the items from the baby shower by the time I returned home from the hospital. I was thankful. It was hard though seeing the nursery that my husband had been working on for months in anticipation of our son's arrival. It was hard seeing baby commercials. It is interesting how as you are going through certain processes things that once seemed inconsequential or small are now a big deal. When I finally started going back to the store, I avoided the baby aisles. It was too painful. Having been pregnant for nearly nine months, I struggled with clothes. Maternity clothes are what fit but they also served as a terrible reminder that I was no longer pregnant and that I did not get to bring my baby home, which was even worse.

I recall the day my breast milk came in. I was not prepared. I think that subconsciously I hoped that since I didn't need it that my body wouldn't make it. But my body didn't know that I didn't need it. I felt terrified and helpless. Seeing pregnant women brought back an array of emotions and I found myself praying for strangers. Praying that their pregnancies would be healthy, fruitful and result in a healthy, living baby. I still pray for pregnant mothers until this day.

Be patient with yourself regarding the outside ouches, whatever they are. Remember you are not a bad person because of the thoughts you have. You are human. You are navigating loss. You are normal. And through it all, you will overcome. You will make it. You will be able to hear of another pregnancy and see another pregnant woman and not want to break down into tears. You will be able to get groceries without being totally consumed by avoiding the baby aisles.

How Long?

How long will it be
Before I can watch TV
And not let its content
Affect me?

How long will it be
Before I can flip through a magazine
Without some ads
Screaming back at me?

How long will it be
Before I can go to the store
And see infants or the infant section
And not head straight for the door?

How long will it be
Before I can see pregnant mothers and smile

And not think so much about
How I lost my child?

How long will it be
Before I can see other babies
And not get sad and upset
And not let it phase me?

How long will it be
Before I can hear other babies coos and cries
And not wonder why
My baby had to die?

How long will it be
Before I can check my email
And it not bother me to see my pregnancy
Described in every detail?

How long will it be
Before I can check my mailbox
And go through magazines, coupons, offers and cards
And not have to stop?

How long? Who knows
Not you, Nor I
But I'll keep believing
It'll get better by and by.

Milk Devastation

Three days after my son's birth
My grief took another turn for the worse

On that Saturday in my bathroom
The moment my breasts sang a startling tune

For I had hoped in all my distress
That my breasts would forget they were breasts

Though I knew Mother Nature is divine
I somehow hoped she'd skip mine

But being a mammal, we take care of our own
So indeed my milk had come, but my baby was gone

The milk I once had anticipated
Had now become the milk I most hated

A constant reminder of what I'd lost
No longer the excitement the idea of nursing had brought

My son had his last meal on the inside of me
My milk would not be needed and that was hard to see

As much as I despised it, I somehow loved it too
It somehow made me feel closer to him and helped to guide me through

So as bad as I wanted it to disappear and go away
A part of me still wished that it could somehow stay

But I had to realize that just couldn't be
The time to nurse my baby hadn't come for me

Through the pain and the suffering
Leaky breasts and horrific engorgement

Though they felt like they would burst
I'd do it all again for my chance to nurse.

You see God does take care of all of His creation
Even in the midst of my Milk Devastation.

Wardrobe Malfunction

Had prepared for four or five more weeks of maternity
Delivering before then had not occurred to me

At least not in the manner that it happened
But it happened the way it happened, unannounced and
without packing

Now an early delivery wouldn't have been so bad
If the ending hadn't been so sad

Leaving me empty, lost, confused and so upset
To leave with empty arms, no baby on my chest

And if that wasn't bad enough
Still looking and feeling pregnant, now that was tough

Pre-maternity clothes just didn't fit
To wear maternity clothes; couldn't fathom it

But I had to anyway
Either that or be naked all day

Couldn't bring myself to go to the store
Had planned to be pregnant just a little while more

Getting a few bigger clothes was the only choice
This made me scream to the top of my voice

Somehow shopping hasn't been the same
The maternity racks still calling my name

Emotionally still pregnant, physically not
Wishing I could make all the pain stop

But the pain and confusion won't stop at this junction
For I'm having a real Wardrobe Malfunction

Poison

I feel like poison, it's strange to say
But it's how I feel anyway

Don't want to be around a pregnant woman for too long
Feel like my presence is just plain wrong

I see the wheels turning within their heads
"I hope my baby doesn't come here dead."

"I hope she doesn't rub off on me."
Then chastise themselves and look at me with sympathy

"I wonder what happened, if they even know why."
"Lord, please don't let my baby die."

Conversations shallow and just plain dry
But I don't wish this on them, why should they have to cry

My presence makes them uncomfortable, just like it makes me
For seeing them recalls my painful memories

Especially with the ones who were pregnant along with you
You used to laugh and talk but now what do you do

Thick unspoken tension, you could cut it with a knife
I hate to be around them, no one should imagine my strife

When I come in contact with them, I wish I could disappear
I just don't want to cause them reason to fear

Lord knows I wish their baby life; He knows I want the best
But I sometimes feel they think I'd rather it be them than me in this mess

Now don't misunderstand, I wanted my baby living here
But because he's not doesn't make me wish death on their dear

Though once they have them the awkwardness somewhat fades
Relief present on their faces since their creation on earth stays

Thank goodness my poison stayed in tact
They have joy instead of pain and I'm happy for that

Then there are the pregnant ones you don't know who want to
hold conversation
Which have you thinking to yourself, "Don't make me relive my
devastation"

But nevertheless the questions come anyway
"Do you have children?" What should I say?

Never been one to discount my son
And the poor mother has no idea what she has done

I reply "one" and pray that they're through
But here they come again, "Is he one or two?"

But I can't blame them, for I too was very excited
But I now see things differently since I was so slighted

My mind's saying there's no way I'm telling this PREGNANT
woman my son's dead
I'd feel like that poison's seeping out to rear its ugly head

I don't want to cause them fear
Ok Lord, please help me here

How can I evade the questions and not cause her pain
Pray for guidance, feign a sneeze and then a quick subject change

So I feel like a poison, it's strange to say
But that's how I feel anyway.

Just Like That

A woman said the strangest thing to me the other day
"Be glad he died before you knew him."
Now what was that to say?

I tried to be calm and politely respond for this was an elderly lady
I told her I knew him and that I had grew him
For he was my baby

She was really trying to be helpful when she said
"I mean you weren't very attached."
He was the life I helped create who lived inside my womb, what's
more attached than that?!

But of course I didn't yell this at her
But simply acknowledged
Our views differ

Tried not to show it on my face
But in my mouth
I had a bad, bad taste

Seems like I'd be used to all this stuff
And that my heart and feelings
Could no longer be crushed

But like the water on a duck's back
I had to let it roll off
Just like that

TRUST ANYWAY

I am a woman of faith. I love Jesus and strive to live as He did but my loss experience tested everything I thought I knew about God. My faith was shattered. I lost my baby and my mom during the same year. I thought that I was being punished. God could not possibly love me. What had I done wrong? What kind of love is this? I had so many questions. For a while, I stopped praying consciously but couldn't turn it off in my subconscious as it was such a big part of me. I struggled to read my Bible. Life just wasn't the same. But just because I left God did not mean that He left me. He was there even when I did not realize it or accept it. Though I still don't understand why He allowed me to get pregnant and birth a lifeless baby, I am leaning on scripture that tells me to lean not unto my own understanding and that His ways are not my ways. I do believe that He has allowed good to come out of my situation as others have found healing and gotten help through my experience. Through it all, He kept me and I know He loves me. I never subscribed to the notion that you can't question God. That's not true and it is not biblical. What child can't ask their father questions? Ask what you want to ask. Say what you want to say. He's a big, big Father and He can handle it and loves us no matter what. It may take time, but you will get there. God will be waiting when you are ready and when you look back on it, I bet that you will see that He never left in the midst of it all.

KNOW

Know what you say when you pray
Oh Lord, have thine own way

Know what you mean when you sing
God, do what's best for me

Know what can happen when you recite
All my battles He will fight

Know that it won't all be fun
When you say your will, not mine be done

Know that it can be misunderstood
When He says all things work together for good

Know that a night of weeping can be more than a dusk till dawn
And the morning that's coming can take very long

Know that just because love is patient, love is kind
It doesn't seem like it all the time

Know that while it's your path He directs
It may lead some places you least expect

Know that when in Him you trust and obey because there's
no other way
That there are some times you will be in dismay

Know that when He says He'll give you your heart's desire
That when it seems different to you it doesn't make Him a liar

Know that though He says I'll be with you always
Doesn't mean you won't have bad days

Know what you believe when you say you are a Christian
Because pain and persecution come with the mission

For everyday won't be sunshine
Because on this walk will be rain sometimes

And even what seems like one million winters
And though you may not see it, God is in the center

For it's during these times God allows you to grow
And even though we don't like it, He allows it to be so

And sometimes it's hard to understand
But we must somehow now trust that He holds the plan

The plan that will lead to joy after the nights
For time to come again when your days can be bright

And if the storm should come again
It's only on Him we can depend

Have You Ever Seen an Angel?

Have you ever seen an angel?

There once was one who came for a while
And all who knew him, hearts did smile

But back to heaven he had to go
For a reason that only God knows

Even though I'm sad and angry, I understand too...
If I was God I'd chosen him too...

Three Aunts

I have three aunts whom I adore
They've traveled down my road before

Two my mom's sisters, one my dad's
All lost a son that they too once had

As a matter of fact, one lost two
And with the Lord's help she still made it through

Don't want to fear our next pregnancy
Which I guess explains some of the reluctancy

Nevertheless, from them I draw strength
Great advice and encouragement from them I can depend

To them, this happened decades ago
And since that time they have other kids to show

Not that one child can replace another
Because a mother's heart still has a void for the other

Though I imagine the comfort it gives
To know the fruit of your womb can live

I look at my aunts and I am relieved
Because each of them have living seeds

They are survivors of their strife
They give me confidence as I fight

Their strength, guidance and example have helped carry
me through
I thank them, love them and cherish them too

Aunt Hurdis, Aunt Gale and Aunt Joe
I thank God for you in ways you'll never know.

He's a Keeper

As I look back over life's recent transpirations
I begin to thank God without hesitation

It was only because He was keeping me close
That I didn't completely lose control

Normal, perfect and moving on Sunday
Before drastic changes occurred on Monday

Just two days after the baby shower
My son lived his final hours

Noticed he wasn't moving that much
Didn't respond to a certain touch

Sitting in my room, started to worry
But tried not to be hasty or act in a hurry

Talked to my husband and the doctor too
Performed a few tests but nothing would do

A few moments later, my mom walked in
I explained my concerns and the prayers began

Before I knew it, my two aunts came
Gave me tea to drink and called Jesus' name

Meanwhile, I waited for the doctor to phone
And of course my hubby had already left home

Then the doctor called and said, "Come and get checked"
I managed to remain calm and tried not to fret

But my doctor was in Birmingham an hour and half away
So I had to go to Montgomery and God would make a way

Aunt Gale took me to the hospital while Aunt Hurdis
stayed with mom
She made some calls along the way and I prayed for my son

She managed to find Dr. Johnson with the help of Uncle Claude
And he came immediately though it was late and all

See, he was the OB of much of my family
Now he had become the doctor for my baby and me

The nurses there admitted me right away
And in the bed I had to lay

Uncle Bob and Aunt Anna by then had come
To offer prayers and support for me and my son

Then my husband appeared out of thin air
Had driven as if Birmingham was no where from there

Then the nurses started to run tests
But no signs of a heartbeat and I was beyond stressed

Kept willing my heart to make his heart beat
Asked for God's help with this enormous feat

One Doppler, then another and an ultrasound too
He didn't move and I was thinking, "this can't be true"

Then the doc did an exam and gave the terrible news
Our son had died in utero and there was nothing we could do

At that moment I had to ask if it was a possibility that
he'd reawake
I'm sorry, but it's not was all he could say

Then it was as if a hurricane appeared
Hubby and I hugged and shed an ocean of tears

But even still, I still had hope
That this was one cruel, cruel joke

Then the doctor stated our plan of action
I'd stay in the hospital and he'd start contractions

He explained that he'd induce labor
And I kept thinking, "Father, come save us."

C-section not an option, would be a regular delivery
I was still willing myself through this misery

More family came but I didn't say much
Trying to remain sane and wrap my mind around this stuff

Doc had prescribed a pill for induction
Had also prescribed others to help me function

Rejected the sleeping and anxiety pills
Didn't have to take them against my will

Still hoping and praying that life would come back
So didn't want to do anything to jeopardize that

By now I'd been moved to a birth suite
At 35 weeks didn't think here I'd be

Lying there hoping he would start to move
And that this was a nightmare that would be over soon

Was told to try to get a good night's rest
But that was impossible with this stress

The next day came and somehow I managed
To still be in place though my heart was panicked

The induction process started and I held on to hope
I believe that was the only way I was able to cope

It was time for me to have the epidural done
I didn't want it, but I still got one

Half numb, half not
Basically how my heart felt in this spot

Time came to deliver and doc was there
So was my family who I hold so dear

My son came out and he looked whole
Except he had already lost his soul

No cry, no movement, no blinking of his eyes
I just lay and watch until I started to cry

He didn't wake up like I hoped he would
My heart was crushed, none of this was good

I held him, I smelled him, I counted his toes
He was perfect and handsome with a cute button nose

When the time came for me to be discharged
I left the hospital but without part of my heart

My arms were empty and so was my soul
All I felt was despair and a big, tremendous hole

Nevertheless, I made it. Somehow I survived
I recognize I could not have done it without God on my side

I know it seems strange to say but I blamed God too
Because He already knew what He was going to allow me to go through

I didn't understand why and I don't until this day
But I know that it is because of Him that I am still here today

He's a keeper, even if His will we don't understand
He's a keeper, even when we don't agree with His plan

He's a keeper through the grief and the despair
Even when I don't feel like it is true, I know that He was always there

MILESTONES & HOLIDAY HOPE

Holidays were the hardest, especially the first ones. My baby was due in March, so I was already looking forward to a cute little Easter basket that I knew my mother would be sure to make. Plus, Mother's Day was going to follow not too long after Easter. Instead of things going how I imagined they would, I spent those days melancholy and reminiscent. Mother's Day was especially hard because I went to church with my mom because it was still Mother's Day for her.

At church, Mother's Day is a big deal. Mothers are recognized and given gifts! I was full of emotion when one of the church members remembered that I too was a mother of an angel baby. Whew! So many emotions. Nevertheless, I survived those holidays and the ones that came after. You will too. You may still have thoughts of what the holidays would have been like with your little one. That is normal. You will have the same thoughts regarding his/her birthday too. Sometimes imagining what could have been is therapeutic and a part of living your process.

One Month Today

Been sitting here wondering
A little extensive pondering

About what you'd be like
If God had postponed your flight

I imagine you squirming and wiggling
Can hear your coos, cries and giggling

Bet you'd be up several times a night
If that were the case, it'd be quite alright

Probably wouldn't like getting your diaper changed
That's ok, sure your daddy was the same

Sure you'd like to eat and eat
And feeding you would've been my treat

Bet you'd like to sleep all day
And get up at night for us to play

Imagine you would've gained a few pounds
Making your little face even more round

Hair fixed up in your wavy, curly fro
Big, dark brown eyes that glow and glow

Probably a little bit darker in skin color
Falling somewhere in between your daddy's and your mother's

Even longer legs and longer little feet
Touching your soft skin sure would mean a lot to me

Wonder what you'd learned and what you'd taught me
You'd be one month today, still wish with us you could be

Easter MoUrning

Had expected Easter; Jesus' resurrection to be your first holiday
Ended up hoping you could be resurrected some way

Had purposefully attended sunrise service
With the hopes of avoiding babies and kids with baskets, outfits,
hats and purses

Didn't really want to hear those cute Easter speeches
Knowing that you'd forever be speechless

Managed to still go to 11 o'clock too
Arrived late so the skits and speeches were through

Left church as soon as it ended
In an effort to keep folks' lips suspended

Took pictures with the family though not feeling photogenic
Just wasn't the same because Walter wasn't in it

I felt lost and found at the same time
My son is gone but Jesus is mine

Joy and sadness covered me together
Like the cloud covering the sun with prospective bad weather

Glad Christ is risen
Though I'm sad for His decision

I made it through Easter MoUrning, from early day till late night
Then on the next day I felt alright.

Mother's Day Journey

I knew when I went to bed on that night
That the next day I'd have to endure with all my might.

Had been preoccupied with my close friend's wedding,
But that was now over and home I was heading.

Not to mention her wedding day happened to be...
My son's three-month funeral anniversary.

Wasn't sure just how I would feel
But with myself I'd made a deal.

To survive Mother's day the best I could
And for myself that'd be good.

Awoke early that morning to a phone call
Uncle Claude on the other end with a pep talk and all.

Made me feel really good; I had not expected it
And my heart did rejoice and I accepted it.

Mom had come up and spent the night
I had her and hubby there to help me with this plight.

Hubby kissed me, held me tight
Reassured me I'd be alright.

Got out of bed, got ready for church
Didn't know what to expect, not expecting too much.

Mom preached a good word and I survived the poems
and speeches
They even gave me a gift bag with a glass and candy pieces.

Made it through the service quite alright
I headed straight for the car until a lady stopped my flight.

She wanted to make sure that I knew
That I was still a mother too.

I said yes ma'am, thanks, I know
Then through the door I did go.

Relieved to be inside the car
A big step for me, I'd come this far.

Buckled up and headed home
With half the day already gone.

We gave mom her gift and she gave me one
Caring and thoughtful, that's my mom.

A lovely card and gift from my hubby
Gift, calls and texts from my closest buddies.

Went to the cemetery to visit my child
Stood, looked, smiled and cried for a while.

Returned to the car and headed to Granny's
Received uneasy looks from my family.

Some had a hard time finding what to say
Some started, then stopped the "Happy Mother's Day."

Received a gift bag from my Aunt
The thought from her meant so very much.

Kissed Granny because we couldn't stay long
But over half the day was already gone.

Back in the car, headed down the street
Uniontown would be my next feat.

We had arrived in plenty of time
They took the silent approach and that was fine.

Fellowshipped, laughed, talked and ate
Then on the road again before it was too late.

It was night by now and we were headed home
And Mother's Day was almost gone!

Hubby and I talked along the way
Arrived at the house and reflected on the day.

Got ready for bed, but before I went to sleep
I kissed my baby's picture, for he was so meek.

Said my prayers and thanked God for His help
He'd held me together in spite of myself.

Closed my eyes, laid on hubby's chest
Mother's Day accomplished now I could rest.

Happy Birthday!

Happy Birthday, my dear son,
Today is the day you would've been one.

If you were here, I imagine you'd be,
Walking, talking and calling daddy.

And though life hasn't been the same since you've been gone,
I know you are just fine in your heavenly home.

And of all the little ones, you're the most blessed of all,
Because you greeted your grandmother when she got her call.

I know you two together are as happy as can be,
 But save some of that singing and playing for your
daddy and me!

So on your birthday, do know you're loved and missed,
And Momma, if you're listening, give him a big birthday kiss.

Our little man—one year on today,

Celebrating in heaven; Happy 1st Birthday!

I hope that you have found this book helpful by being able to relate or understand. I hope that you have been encouraged on your journey and that you will continue to stand. May you find comfort and validation in the words here. I hope that you do not mind me praying for you because I can't help but to. I pray that you have family and friends around you that are understanding. I pray that you find tools to help you heal and cope. I encourage you to seek counseling and therapy as you see fit. You can also consider joining support groups. Most of all, give yourself grace and space to feel what you feel but as you are doing so, don't lose hope. Even if you can't see it, you will make it.

Sincerely,
Coretta

For more information please visit **www.ccthenp.com**